THE PLANETARY SOCIETY

T0112985

URANUS

THE SIDEWAYS PLANET

Bruce Betts, PhD

Lerner Publications ◆ Minneapolis

THE PLANETS AND MOONS IN OUR SOLAR SYSTEM ARE OUT OF THIS WORLD. Some are hotter than an oven, and some are much colder than a freezer. Some are small and rocky, while others are huge and mostly made of gas. As you explore these worlds, you'll discover giant canyons, active volcanoes, strange kinds of ice, storms bigger than Earth, and much more.

The Planetary Society® empowers people around the world to advance space science and exploration. On behalf of The Planetary Society®, including our tens of thousands of members, here's wishing you the joy of discovery.

Onward,

Bill Nye

Bill Nye
CEO, The Planetary Society®

TABLE OF CONTENTS

CHAPTER 1 **The Sideways Planet**   4

CHAPTER 2 **Blue Uranus**   12

CHAPTER 3 **Exploring Uranus**   26

Glossary   30
Learn More   30
Index   31

THE SIDEWAYS PLANET

The Sun is the center of our solar system. There are eight planets, and they all circle the Sun. Uranus is the seventh planet from the Sun.

MEET PLANET URANUS

Uranus looks like a smooth blue ball. It tilts so far to the side that it's known as the sideways planet.

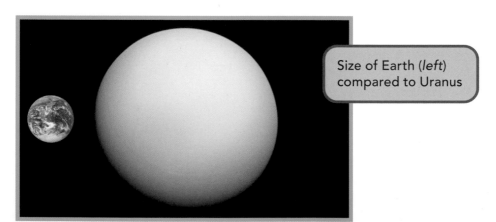

Size of Earth (*left*) compared to Uranus

Uranus is smaller than Saturn, a little larger than Neptune, and much bigger than Earth. About sixty-three Earths could fit inside Uranus. If Earth were the size of a tennis ball, Uranus would be about the size of a basketball.

 URANUS FAST FACTS

Size	Could fit about sixty-three Earths inside Uranus
Distance from the Sun	1.8 billion miles (2.9 billion km)
Length of day	About 17.2 hours
Length of year	About eighty-four Earth years
Number of moons	At least twenty-seven

Days are shorter on Uranus than on Earth. An Earth day is twenty-four hours. But a Uranus day is about seventeen hours. Years on Uranus are longer than years on Earth. One Earth year is about 365 days. But one Uranus year is about eighty-four Earth years.

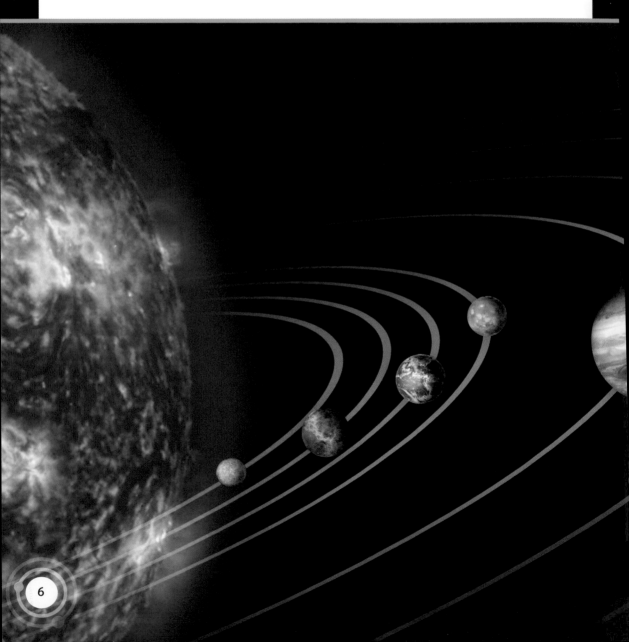

Uranus orbits, or goes around, the Sun between Saturn and Neptune. It is about nineteen times farther from the Sun than Earth is. This distance makes Uranus and its moons much colder than Earth because they get less heat from the Sun.

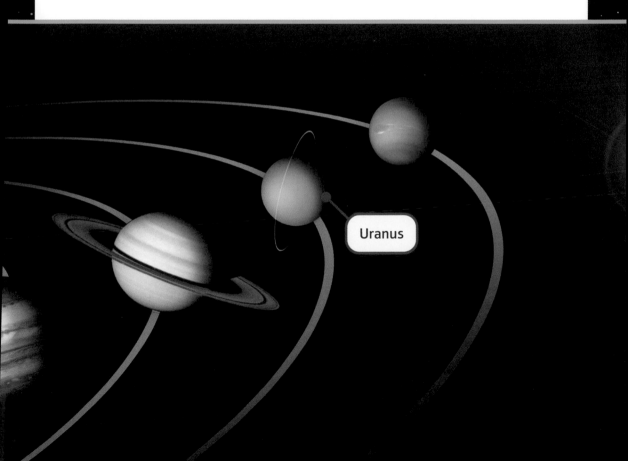

Uranus

GIANT AND ICE PLANETS

The four planets farthest from the Sun are called the outer planets or the giant planets. They are Jupiter, Saturn, Uranus, and Neptune. These planets are much larger than Earth and the other inner, rocky planets.

Uranus and Neptune are also known as ice giants. They are mostly made of things that form ices such as water, ammonia, and methane.

Left to right: Jupiter, Saturn, Uranus, and Neptune are the outer planets in our solar system.

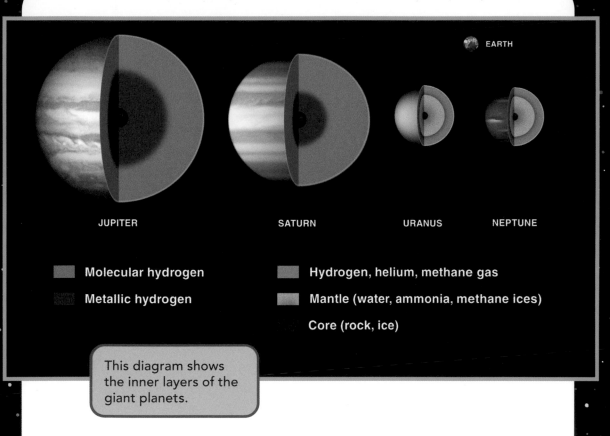

EARTH

JUPITER   SATURN   URANUS   NEPTUNE

Molecular hydrogen   Hydrogen, helium, methane gas

Metallic hydrogen   Mantle (water, ammonia, methane ices)

Core (rock, ice)

This diagram shows the inner layers of the giant planets.

   The outer part of Uranus is all atmosphere. It is mostly made of hydrogen gas. But it also has some helium and methane. Methane is what makes Uranus look blue.

   Uranus has a layer of hot fluids below the outer part. These include water, ammonia, and methane. There is likely a rocky core at the center of the planet.

All the giant planets have rings. But their rings are very different. Saturn's icy rings are the most famous because they're the biggest and easiest to see.

Uranus's rings are very dark, thin, and hard to see. They are a mix of ice, dirt, and rock. Scientists have found thirteen rings around Uranus.

These images show some of Uranus's rings.

Fun Names
Most moons have names from Greek or Roman myths. The moons of Uranus have names from the plays of William Shakespeare or the poetry of Alexander Pope.

Uranus has at least twenty-seven moons. We keep finding more. Five of the moons are large and shaped like balls. The rest are much smaller and come in lots of shapes and sizes. Most of the moons are very dark.

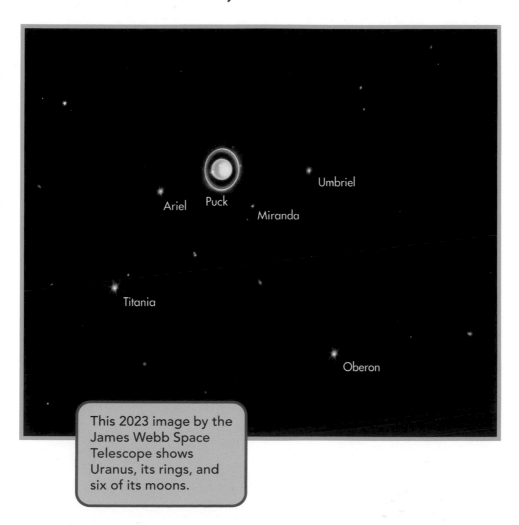

This 2023 image by the James Webb Space Telescope shows Uranus, its rings, and six of its moons.

CHAPTER 2

BLUE URANUS

During parts of the year, you can see Uranus in the sky using binoculars or a telescope. Uranus would look like a small blue circle. With a very dark sky, you might be able to see Uranus with just your eyes. It would look like a faint star.

Scientists use very large telescopes on Earth and in space to see Uranus more clearly. They can see that Uranus is blue and sometimes has clouds. The clouds change over time. Some telescopes can see the rings and many of the moons.

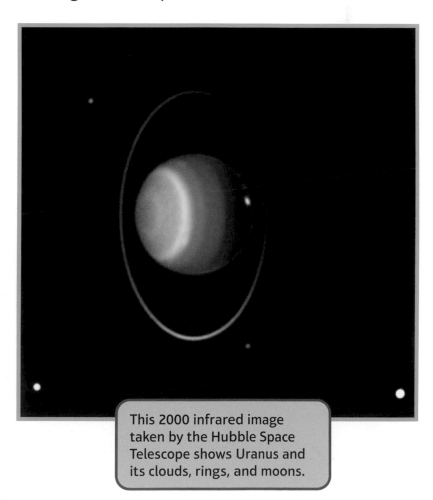

This 2000 infrared image taken by the Hubble Space Telescope shows Uranus and its clouds, rings, and moons.

Uranus the God

Planet Uranus is named after the Greek god of the sky. The Greek god was the father of Cronus (Saturn in Roman myth) and the grandfather of Zeus (Jupiter in Roman myth).

COLOR AND STORMS

The Voyager 2 spacecraft arrived at Uranus in 1986. Voyager 2 saw that Uranus looked like a solid blue ball.

Uranus as seen by Voyager 2

We have built bigger and better Earth and space telescopes since Voyager 2 flew by Uranus. These telescopes often use cameras that can see infrared light. It's a type of light we can't see. Telescopes help us see many storms and more.

An infrared image of cloud stripes and a dark spot on Uranus (*top*) and an infrared image of a bright cloud covering Uranus's north pole (*right*)

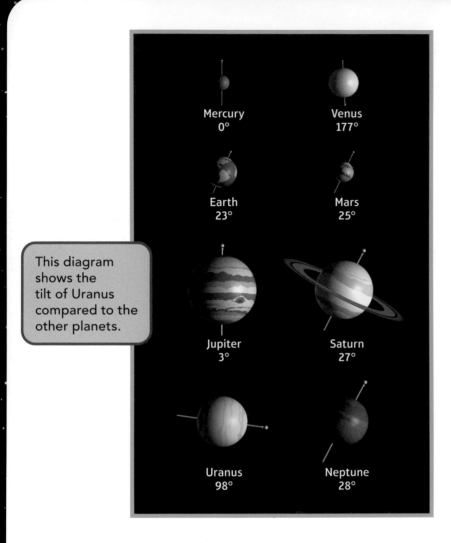

Mercury
0°

Venus
177°

Earth
23°

Mars
25°

Jupiter
3°

Saturn
27°

Uranus
98°

Neptune
28°

This diagram shows the tilt of Uranus compared to the other planets.

EXTREME TILT

Uranus is the only planet tilted on its side. Earth has a small tilt. Earth's tilt is why we have seasons.

When it's summer where you live, that part of Earth is tilted toward the Sun. That part of Earth is tilted away during winter. Summer is warmer than winter because there is more direct sunlight in the summer.

Uranus's tilt is why it has extreme seasons. Each Uranus year, the north pole will point at the Sun for about twenty-one Earth years. The south pole will be in darkness during that time.

Uranus's clouds change with the season. Bright clouds form over the poles at certain times of year when they receive sunlight.

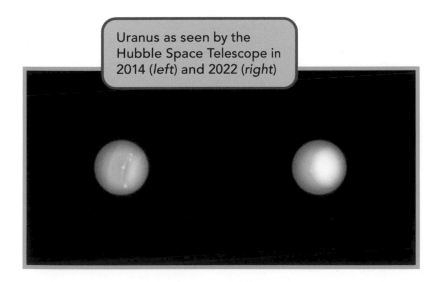

Uranus as seen by the Hubble Space Telescope in 2014 (*left*) and 2022 (*right*)

The Rings

Uranus has thirteen known rings. The first rings were found in 1977 with telescopes. Voyager 2 and the Hubble Space Telescope found more rings in later years.

We see the rings at different angles from Earth because of Uranus's tilt. Every forty-two years, we only see the edges of the rings. That last happened in 2007. Twenty-one years before or after, we see the rings as circles. That happens when one of the poles points toward the Sun.

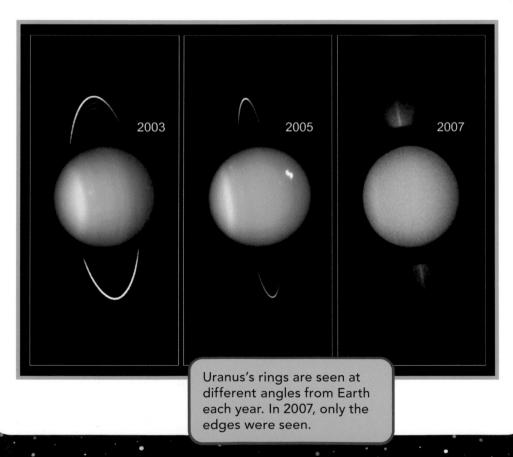

2003   2005   2007

Uranus's rings are seen at different angles from Earth each year. In 2007, only the edges were seen.

The eleven rings closest to Uranus are narrow and dark. They are likely a mix of water ice and dirt. They may have formed from a past breakup of one or more moons. The two rings farther from Uranus are wider and fainter.

Some rings have a tiny moon on each side of the ring. These are called shepherding moons.

Uranus's rings as seen by Voyager 2

Two shepherding moons are seen on the sides of one of Uranus's rings.

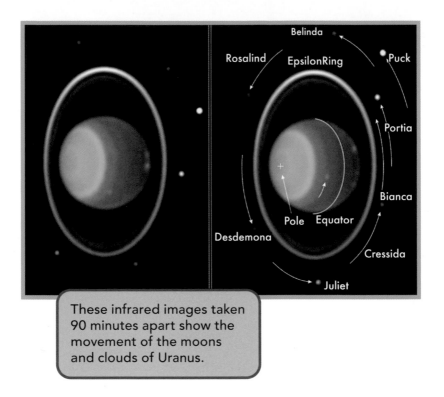

These infrared images taken 90 minutes apart show the movement of the moons and clouds of Uranus.

MANY MOONS

Uranus has five major moons. They are larger than the rest. Scientists think the moons may be made of a mix of water ice and rock. The moons are dark. All our close-up pictures of the moons come from Voyager 2.

Miranda is the smallest and closest of the major moons to Uranus. It is also the strangest. Its surface looks different than any other moon in the solar system. It looks like it was pulled apart and put back together again.

Miranda may have been pulled apart and put back together with a big impact. But something else may have caused Miranda's strange surface.

Verona Rupes on Miranda is the highest cliff in the solar system. It's about 12 miles (20 km) high.

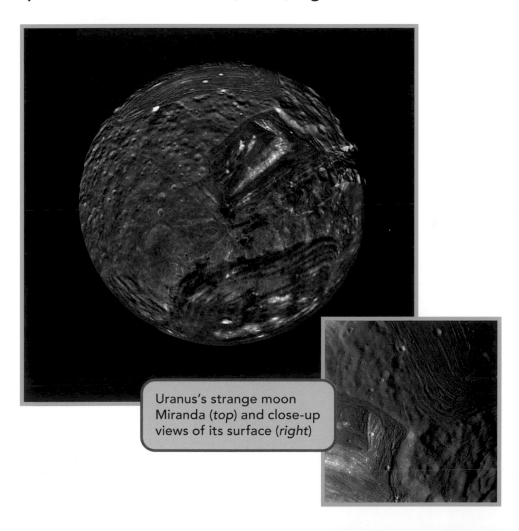

Uranus's strange moon Miranda (*top*) and close-up views of its surface (*right*)

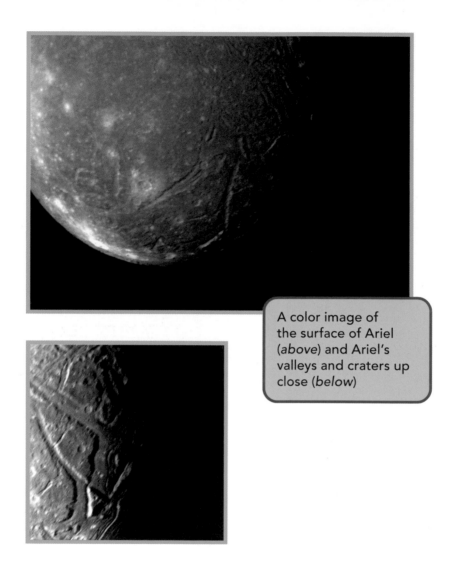

A color image of the surface of Ariel (*above*) and Ariel's valleys and craters up close (*below*)

Ariel is the brightest of the major moons. But it is still very dark. It has valleys and ridges crossing its surface.

Umbriel has an old surface covered in craters. Craters are caused by space rocks hitting a surface at high speeds.

Umbriel is the darkest of the major moons. There is one bright ring at the top. It could be made of things thrown out by an impact of a high-speed space rock. It could also be carbon dioxide ice.

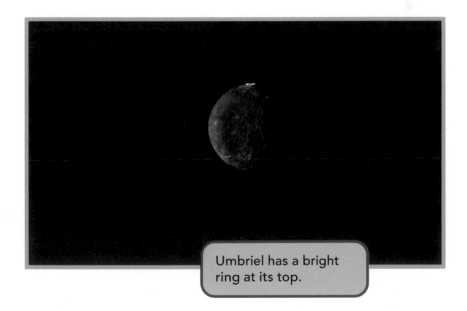

Umbriel has a bright ring at its top.

Titania is the largest moon of Uranus. It is the eighth largest moon in the solar system. But it is much smaller than the seven other large moons. Titania is covered in craters. It also has cracks and canyons.

These images are of Titania. The right image is the moon in color.

A color image of Oberon

The major moon farthest from Uranus is Oberon. Oberon is covered in craters and has an old surface. Older surfaces like Mercury, Earth's Moon, or Oberon have more craters.

EXPLORING URANUS

The giant planets are not near Earth. Spacecraft help us study the planets up close. Voyager 2 is the only spacecraft that has visited Uranus because the planet is so far away.

Voyager 2 launched in 1977. It visited all the giant planets. Our close-up images of Uranus, its moons, and its rings come from Voyager 2's flyby in 1986.

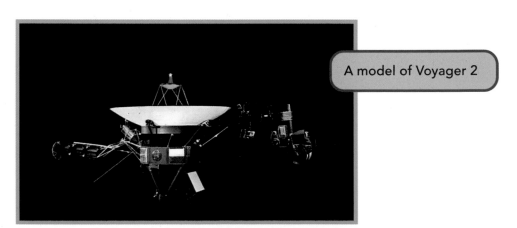

A model of Voyager 2

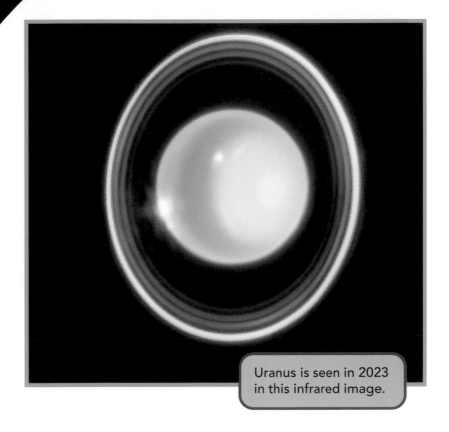

Uranus is seen in 2023 in this infrared image.

THE FUTURE

A spacecraft mission is being planned to go to Uranus. But it will be many years before it launches and many more years before it gets there.

The good news is our telescopes have gotten much better. We can continue to study Uranus from Earth and watch how the planet changes over time.

Uranus as seen from Voyager 2 as the spacecraft flew away from the planet

There will be more to learn about Uranus in the coming years. And that's only one out of the eight planets. Enjoy your journey through the solar system!

A Long Trip
Voyager 2 traveled at tens of thousands of miles per hour. Even though it was fast, it still took nine years to reach Uranus.

Titan IIIE-Centaur, the rocket carrying Voyager 2, launches in 1977.

Glossary

atmosphere: the gases surrounding a planet, moon, or other body

core: the center of a planet or moon

day: the time it takes a planet to spin around and go from noon to noon. One Earth day is about twenty-four hours.

flyby: a spacecraft's flight passing by a planet for observation

planet: a big, round, ball-shaped object that only goes around the Sun. Our solar system has eight planets. A planet does not have anything close to the same size near its orbit.

spacecraft: a vehicle or object made for travel in outer space

tilt: how much something such as a planet leans sideways

year: the time it takes a planet to go all the way around the Sun. One Earth year is about 365 days.

Learn More

Betts, Bruce, PhD. *Neptune: Planet of Wind and Ice.* Minneapolis: Lerner Publications, 2025.

Britannica Kids: Uranus
https://kids.britannica.com/kids/article/Uranus/353890

Golusky, Jackie, *Explore Uranus.* Minneapolis: Lerner Publications, 2021.

Mazzarella, Kerri. *Uranus.* Coral Springs, FL: Seahorse, 2023.

NASA Space Place: All about Uranus
https://spaceplace.nasa.gov/all-about-uranus/en/

The Planetary Society: Uranus, the Sideways Planet
https://www.planetary.org/worlds/Uranus

Index

atmosphere, 9

core, 9

giant planets, 8, 10, 26

moons, 5, 7, 10–11, 13, 19–26

Neptune, 5, 7–8

rings, 10, 13, 18–19, 26

tilt, 4

Voyager 2, 14–15, 18, 20, 26, 28

Photo Acknowledgments

Image credits: NASA (modified by Jcpag2012), p. 4; NASA/JPL, p. 6–7, 10 (both); 19 (both); 21 (right), 22 (both), 23, 24 (both), 25, 28; NASA, p. 8, 9, 26; NASA, ESA, CSA, STScI; image processing: J. DePasquale (STScI), pp. 11, 27; Jon Hicks/Getty Images, p. 12; NASA/JPL/STScI, pp. 13, 15 (left); 20; NASA/JPL-Caltech, p. 14; NASA, ESA, A. Simon (NASA-GSFC), and M.H. Wong and A. Hsu (UC Berkeley), pp. 15 (right); NASA/JPL-Caltech/Richard Barkus, p. 16; NASA, ESA, STScI, A. Simon (NASA-GSFC), Michael H. Wong (UC Berkeley), p. 17; NASA, ESA, and M. Showalter (SETI Institute), p. 18; NASA/JPL/USGS, p. 21 (left); NASA/MSFC, p. 29; Design elements: Sergey Balakhnichev/Getty Images; Baac3nes/Getty Images; Elena Kryulena/Shutterstock; Anna Frajtova/Shutterstock.
Cover: NASA/JPL-Caltech.

FOR MY SONS, KEVIN AND DANIEL, AND FOR ALL THE MEMBERS OF THE PLANETARY SOCIETY®

Lerner Publications Company
An imprint of Lerner Publishing Group, Inc.
241 First Avenue North
Minneapolis, MN 55401 USA

For reading levels and more information, look up this title at www.lernerbooks.com.

Main body text set in Aptifer Sans LT Pro. Typeface provided by Linotype AG.

Editor: Brianna Kaiser **Designer:** Mary Ross
Lerner team: Connie Kuhnz

Library of Congress Cataloging-in-Publication Data

Names: Betts, Bruce (PhD), author.
Title: Uranus : the sideways planet / Bruce Betts, PhD.
Description: Minneapolis, MN : Lerner Publications, [2025] | Series: Exploring our solar system with the Planetary Society | Includes bibliographical references and index. | Audience: Ages 7–10 | Audience: Grades 2–3 | Summary: "With seasons that last for decades, Uranus is a planet of extremes. Young readers explore the seventh planet from the Sun through fun facts, tables, and colorful photographs"— Provided by publisher.
Identifiers: LCCN 2023048846 (print) | LCCN 2023048847 (ebook) | ISBN 9798765626870 (library binding) | ISBN 9798765628676 (paperback) | ISBN 9798765633403 (epub)
Subjects: LCSH: Uranus (Planet)—Juvenile literature.
Classification: LCC QB681 .B488 2025 (print) | LCC QB681 (ebook) | DDC 523.47—dc23/eng/20231117

LC record available at https://lccn.loc.gov/2023048846
LC ebook record available at https://lccn.loc.gov/2023048847

Manufactured in the United States of America
1-1010103-52018-2/22/2024